Copyright © 2017 by Dr. Douglas Peake

Unless otherwise indicated, all Scripture quotations are taken from The Holy Bible, New International Version©, NIV©. Copyright 1973, 1978, 1984, 2011 by Biblica, Inc. © Used by permission. All rights reserved worldwide.

All rights reserved. No part of this publication may be reproduced, stored in a retrieval system, or transmitted in any form or by any means - electronic, mechanical, photocopy, recording, or any other – except for brief quotations in printed reviews, without the author's permission.

ISBN 979-8-9989239-0-6

Introduction

The Bible is the greatest book known in human history. It has sold more copies than any other book since the beginning of time, been translated into more languages than any other book, and has impacted nations and empires more than any other book...... **in history**! Now, that is a pretty bold statement! I state it because it is true. There are many reasons it has been so influential: its historical accuracy, authenticity, archeological factual content, theme, and description of human nature.

The Bible has many critics. It has been attacked, misused, quoted out of context, shredded, banned, burned, and manipulated more than any other book in human history.

What makes the Bible such a controversial book? It might be because of its claims. The Bible calls itself the revelation of God. It is said to outline God's plan for humanity at both the beginning and end of history. It claims to be a complete revelation, meaning there is no need for any other religious books. These are lofty claims for a book filled with interesting characters, ancient customs, a culture that doesn't exist, and written in a language few can understand.

How can a person read the Bible, believe it to be true and accurate, and understand it completely?

This booklet is designed to help you read and understand the Bible. As you progress through this book, you'll develop a frame of reference that serves as a guide to show you where to begin your exploration of the Bible. Having a solid frame of reference is crucial for comprehending the text; it influences how you interpret what you read and determines whether you see its relevance in your life or dismiss it altogether.

To understand the Bible, it's essential to start by understanding yourself. This doesn't require a complete self-analysis, but you should recognize that your initial perspective will shape your experience with the scripture.

Throughout this book, you will discover the Bible's remarkable consistency. You'll see the historical evidence supporting its authenticity, the archaeological findings that attest to its truth, and the Bible's ability to withstand scrutiny.

Most importantly, this book is intended for you. Your faith journey with Jesus Christ is a vital part of your identity, and this book aims to demonstrate how the Bible is a gift from God meant to strengthen your faith.

I have three main goals for this book. First, I want to help you develop the best possible frame of reference so that you can fully engage with the Bible and avoid frustration. Second, I want to assure you that even if you do not accept the claims made in the Bible, the historical facts, geographical locations, and its overall authenticity are highly reliable. You can trust that it is true. Finally, I aim to guide you to the best starting point for your journey. Rather than wandering aimlessly, begin with the central figure of the story: Jesus.

Chapter One: How Remarkable Is The Bible?

The entire Bible functions as a library of books that span a vast amount of time. If you were to read the Bible like any regular book, it would take some time and effort to digest. However, you would uncover a common theme running throughout, from the Old Testament to the New Testament. This theme is particularly remarkable when you consider that the Bible is made up of 66 smaller books written over a period of approximately 1,500 years by 40 different authors. Most of these authors never met each other, nor did they read each other's works. This scenario might seem ripe for confusion and contradiction, yet the Bible's theme remains remarkably unified, allowing it to be understood as a single coherent text.

The Bible is also remarkable because people have believed it to be the word of God for 2,000 years. It has significantly influenced history, science, nations, and individuals. In today's world, filled with technology, data, science, and an abundance of skepticism, we must ask: Is it still possible to view the Bible as the word of God?

This question is what we aim to explore in this book.

It would be simple to write a book filled with claims about the Bible, hoping that you accept them as true, which is akin to preaching to the choir since they already believe. But what about those who have questions, skepticism, or uncertainty? The goal here is to compare the Bible with other ancient texts that exist today, both sacred and non-sacred. We want to answer the question: When the Bible is put alongside these other ancient texts and examined under the same academic rigor, how does its authenticity and integrity hold up?

Genuine scholarship welcomes scrutiny and inquiry. It is crucial to ask these questions about the Bible because they pertain to your life. You have only one life; is it based on truth or falsehood? All sacred texts have gained their status because they seek to answer the fundamental question: "Why are you here?" Each sacred text provides a unique answer to this inquiry. Reflect on this: "Which sacred text should I believe to understand the meaning and purpose of my life?"

Finding your answer to this question can mean the difference between a life well-lived and one filled with confusion and disappointment.

Let's begin our journey by exploring the major belief systems of the world today and their corresponding sacred texts. When you distill it down, you will find there are only five sacred texts currently in existence:

1. **The Tanakh**: The Jewish Bible. The first five books, known as the Pentateuch, are attributed to Moses, who led the Israelites across the Sinai desert into the Promised Land. There are additional texts, but it essentially comprises the Old Testament.

2. **The Qur'an**: The holy book of Islam, written in the 6th century. It records the visions of Mohammed, referred to as Al

Qur'an, which translates to "Recitation." Mohammed is said to have recited what he was told in these visions, which he claims originated from Allah.

3. **The Vedas**: The holy writings of Hinduism, considered some of the oldest sacred texts, dating back to 1,500-1,000 BC. Because they originated as oral recitations, authorship remains unknown, as they were later written down by various individuals and assembled over time.

4. **The Tripitaka**: The holy writings of Buddhism, literally meaning "Three Baskets." The three baskets encompass the teachings of Buddha, monastic regulations, and ethical instructions.

5. **The Christian Bible**: Comprising 66 books divided into two sections—the Old Testament (or Old Revelation) and the New Testament (or New Revelation). The Bible narrates the story of God's love and redemption for humankind.

How do these five sacred texts compare? If you were to evaluate them based on historical accuracy, geographical integrity, authenticity of statements, and conceptual unity, what conclusions would you draw?

I have previously shared my thoughts through blogging and podcasting under the Salty Pasture moniker, with the motto: "I'm not here to tell you what to think but to help you think for yourself." The aim of this book is to assist you in drawing your own conclusions.

It may not seem significant, but this principle is crucial. What I think about the Bible is irrelevant to your life. My opinions—regardless of how well-researched and logical they may be—will not affect the quality of the life you lead. What truly matters is what you believe about the Bible and what you consider true or false. I have always believed that individuals should have the freedom to form their own opinions. A reasoned choice ultimately has the most significant impact on your life.

By employing methods of objective evaluation, I hope to enable you to make your own confident conclusions. The purpose of using objective evaluation methods is to minimize personal bias as much as possible and to level the playing field, meaning we should apply the same standards of scrutiny across all texts.

Chapter Two: How do I know what I am reading is true?

The first objective evaluation of every ancient document is to ask the question: "How did it get here?"

You can walk into any large bookstore chain or go online to Amazon.com and buy a copy of Homer's Iliad (a poem about the Battle of Troy and Achilles). The Iliad is believed to have been written approximately 800 years before Christ was born (2,800 years ago) and written in a language that hasn't been spoken in centuries. In universities across the land, professors teach about Homer, and the battle he recorded, in his epic poem. There are maps and graphics representing the city of Troy. Models of the Trojan Horse sit on tables in classrooms. Does anyone ever ask the question: "How do you now there is a Homer, who actually wrote about a battle? How do you know there was a walled city named Troy and how do you know the battle took place? How do you know the characters of Achilles, Agamemnon and Odysseus were real people?

These can be tough facts to verify, especially when you realize there are no original manuscripts of Homer's Iliad. As a matter of fact, the earliest manuscript in existence is dated 1,000 AD., 1,800 years after the battle supposedly took place! However, none of the universities question the "believability" of Homer's Iliad. Professors who teach on this subject start with the premise that it is authentic.

Regarding other sacred texts, scholars also accept them as believable even though there are no original manuscripts available to study.

For instance, there are no original manuscripts for the Bible, the Qur'an, the Vedas, The Tripitaka, The Book of Mormon, or the Shakespearean plays and yet scholars accept them as authentic. Whenever they teach on one of these ancient texts they start from the premise that these ancient texts are authentic. How do they come to this conclusion?

It is all about the process.

Over the centuries, scholars have developed a process to determine the authenticity of ancient documents. Similar to the rules of evidence, when the process is followed, documents have a certain level of credibility. The greater the success throughout the process, the greater the credibility.

The process is similar to the scientific process for discovering illness. For instance, when someone goes to the doctor and the doctor says, "You have a problem with your appendix, it needs to come out." How do you know the doctor is telling you the truth? Have you ever seen an appendix? Do you know what it does? If you are asleep when the procedure takes place, how do you know the surgeon actually removed it? What if there is an "appendix" conspiracy out there where doctors say this just to make money?

You believe what the doctor is telling you because you trust the doctors. Why do you trust the doctors? Because there is a **process** that has emerged through the history of modern medicine that has proven the symptoms you have are caused by a small thing called an "appendix." The process includes certain tests that confirm the doctor's diagnosis that your appendix is the problem. The process is one that has been developed over decades of practice. On occasion, it can be wrong but the vast majority of the time the process is highly accurate. Therefore, you trust the doctor and have your appendix removed.

In the same manner, when determining the authenticity of ancient documents, there is a process that can be trusted. It has been developed throughout centuries of usage and is highly accurate. What is strange is that when critics, skeptics, nay-sayers and atheists attack the authenticity of the Bible, they do so by attacking the process. If they can discredit the process, then it appears there is a rational, or "scientific" basis for discrediting the Bible. In the end, they are simply destroying a process for all ancient documents. The result of their efforts is not reasonable or scientific at all. If you employed their process, it would undermine the authenticity of all ancient documents. No one could believe any of the documents were ever authentic. The fact is that the Bible is able to go through the process for all ancient documents and emerge as the leader in authenticity. Therefore, if the Bible is discredited by the process, then none of the other ancient documents stand a chance.

So why should you even care about the process for determining authenticity? It's all about trust. Let's go back to our doctor. Why do you trust her? Is it because she is nice, looks good in a white lab coat, or because she wears interesting shoes? No, you trust her because of the process. The process that determines whether or not she is educated and experienced enough to be licensed as a doctor. You also trust the process in which a medical diagnosis is made. Therefore, if there is no ability to trust in a process to determine authenticity, then there is no process to trust for determining anything- which puts us back in the ice age. If I haven't convinced you yet that there is a process that is effective; then let's describe the process so you can make your own judgment. The process to determine authenticity begins with these questions:

1. What are the earliest manuscripts that we have of this document?

2. When was it claimed to have been written?

3. Who claims to have written it?

4. Is there any other writings or archeological evidence that show the person who claims to have wrote it existed?

5. Is there any other writings or archeological evidence which show that the events in the document really happened?

Each of these questions is designed to described the process used to determine authenticity of ancient documents. On the following page is a chart of all the ancient texts we have mentioned up to this point and how they rate according to the process for determining their authenticity.

Document:	Homer's Iliad	Qur'an	Vedas	Tripitaka	Book of Mormon	The Bible
Claims written:	800 BC	610-653 AD	1500-1000 BC	500 BC	2500-400 BC	1500 BC-90AD
Earliest Manuscripts	1000 AD (1800 yr. gap)	1500 AD (500 yr. gap)	1150 AD (2,000 yr. gap)	1900 AD (2600 yr gap)	None exist	OT 150 BC (1,000 yr. gap) NT 90 AD (30 yr. gap)
Number of Manuscripts	643	too few to count	disputed	none exist	none exist	5,000

Homer's Iliad. The battle he recorded in his epic poem is well-known, and there are maps and graphics representing the city of Troy. Models of the Trojan Horse sit on tables in classrooms. Yet, has anyone ever asked the question: "How do you know there was a Homer who actually wrote about a battle? How do you know there was a walled city named Troy, and how do you know the battle took place? How do you know the characters Achilles, Agamemnon, and Odysseus were real people?"

These can be challenging facts to verify, especially when you realize there are no original manuscripts of Homer's "Iliad." In fact, the earliest manuscript in existence is dated 1,000 AD, which is 1,800 years after the battle supposedly took place! Despite this, universities do not question the "believability" of Homer's "Iliad." Professors teaching on the subject start with the premise that it is authentic.

Similarly, scholars accept other sacred texts as believable, even though none of them have original manuscripts available for study. For instance, there are no original manuscripts for the Bible, the Qur'an, the Vedas, the Tripitaka, the Book of Mormon, or the Shakespearean plays, yet scholars still regard them as authentic. When teaching these ancient texts, they begin with the assumption that these texts are indeed authentic. But how do they come to this conclusion?

It all comes down to process.

Over the centuries, scholars have developed a method for determining the authenticity of ancient documents. This process is akin to the rules of evidence; when the process is followed, documents are granted a certain level of credibility. The greater the success throughout the process, the higher the credibility.

The process resembles the scientific method for diagnosing illness. For example, when someone goes to the doctor and is told, "You have a problem with your appendix, and it needs to be removed," how do you know the doctor is telling the truth? Have you ever seen an appendix? Do you understand its function? If you are unconscious during the procedure, how can you be sure the surgeon actually removed it? What if there's a conspiracy where doctors claim appendectomies are necessary just to make money?

You trust what the doctor tells you because you trust doctors in general. Why do you trust them? Because a process has emerged through modern medicine, proven over time, that confirms your symptoms are caused by that small organ called the "appendix." This process includes specific tests that verify the doctor's diagnosis. Although on occasion it can be wrong, the accuracy is high, which is why you trust the doctor and consent to the surgery.

In a similar fashion, when determining the authenticity of ancient documents, there is a reliable process that has been fine-tuned over centuries and has demonstrated high accuracy. What is surprising is that when critics, skeptics, and atheists challenge the authenticity of the Bible, they often attack the process itself.

If they can discredit the process, it may seem that there is a rational or "scientific" basis for discrediting the Bible. Ultimately, however, they are undermining the process for all ancient documents. Their actions do not yield reasonable or scientific conclusions; rather, if one were to apply their method broadly, it would cast doubt on the authenticity of all ancient writings.

The reality is that the Bible can successfully undergo the process for evaluating ancient documents and emerge as a leader in authenticity. Consequently, if the Bible is deemed invalid by this process, then all other ancient documents are similarly jeopardized.

So why should you care about the process for determining authenticity? It's all about trust. Let's revisit the example of the doctor. Why do you trust her? Is it because she is pleasant, looks good in a white lab coat, or wears stylish shoes? No, you trust her because of the established process. This process determines whether she is educated and experienced enough to be licensed as a doctor. You also have confidence in the process by which a medical diagnosis is made. If there is no reliable way to assess authenticity, then we cannot trust any process for determining truth— which would effectively take us back to a more primitive state.

If I haven't yet convinced you of the effectiveness of this process, then let me outline it so you can make your own judgment. The process to determine authenticity begins with these questions:
1. What are the earliest manuscripts we have of this document?
2. When was it claimed to have been written?
3. Who claims to have written it?

4. Is there any other writing or archaeological evidence that verifies the existence of the person who claimed authorship?

5. Is there additional writing or archaeological evidence that supports the events documented?

Each of these questions is designed to elaborate on the process used to assess the authenticity of ancient documents.

The Process

The following process has been applied with great scrutiny to the Bible. As a matter of fact, the Bible has survived greater scrutiny than any other ancient document known to mankind. Let's look at some specific steps applied to all documents of antiquity and how the Bible compares.

Step 1- Are there any original manuscripts or copies? At this time, there are no original manuscripts for the Iliad, Plato's Republic, any of Shakespeare's plays, the Vedas, the Qur'an, The Book of Mormon, or the Bible. Therefore, the manuscripts that are copies of the originals become very important. The quality of these copies give scholars the confidence to accept ancient documents as authentic. If the copies are credible then Shakespeare's plays, Homer's Iliad, and Plato's Republic are authentic. Therefore, if the quality of the New Testament manuscripts exceed those of the other sacred texts, as well as Homer's Iliad, Shakespeare's plays and Plato's Republic, then logic would dictate that the Bible (if these other documents are accepted as authentic) is authentic as well.

As the chart on page 13 shows, the Bible has more copies available to study than any other ancient document. The quality of these copies far exceeds the quality of many other copies of ancient documents.

Step 2- How close are the manuscripts (which are copies of originals) to the originals? The time gap between when the originals were written and the existing copies determines the accuracy of transmission. In other words, if there are centuries between the copies in existence and the actual time when they were written, possibilities for mistakes grow exponentially. The shorter the time span, the more accurate the copy.
As you can see in the chart on page 13, the Bible has one of the shortest time gaps between when the originals were claimed to have been written and the actual manuscripts we have to study.

Step 3- Are there any ancient writings that quote the original New Testament? One important step that gives tremendous credibility to an ancient document is if there is another, separate ancient document that mentions its existence. What is even more dramatic is when one ancient document actually quotes another ancient document. This is similar to having numerous witnesses testifying to the same thing- it gives overwhelming credibility to the document.

When it comes to the New Testament, not only are there over 5,000 manuscripts dating close to the originals, there are also writings from early church father's who quoted the New Testament in their writings. 95% of the New Testament is quoted in the writings of the early Church fathers- some quotes penned as early as 110 AD.

Step 4 – How did authors who quoted the New Testament perceive the scriptures texts they quoted? This is a very rare step to take but a significant one. It is rare because in order for you to use this step, the ancient document must have been quoted in other ancient documents with different authors. If in fact the document reaches this stage, one must ask the question: "How did these other authors perceive this ancient document?" When studying ancient texts that mention or quote the Bible, all of the authors viewed the scriptures they quoted as the revelation of God. They treated these writings as sacred.

The significance of this step removes any doubt in the mind of a rational person that the Bible is an authentic document and that from the beginning it was considered sacred.

Chapter 3: Myths and Other Legends

There is always a conspiracy theory. They key is discovering how you can know something to be true or false. Once a person begins to see and understand the process that all scholars use to determine the authenticity of ancient documents you discover how you can know whether something is true or false. Furthermore, when you discover how the Bible surpasses all other documents held up to this process, they begin to see how easy it is to see through myths and legends concerning the Bible. The following are myths that have become popular in the last few decades.

Council of Nicaea A popular myth that has circulated in today's world is the belief that the early Christian church invented the Bible during a council convened early in the reign of the Roman Emperor Constantine. This myth has gained traction, particularly due to certain fictional works that Hollywood adapted into movies.

However, this assertion is completely false.

What actually occurred at this council is well documented in historical writings and has no relation to the myth. The council was convened by Constantine, the Emperor of Rome, in the town of Nicaea in Bithynia (modern-day Turkey) in 325 AD. This event is now known as the Council of Nicaea.

The myth suggests that Emperor Constantine convened this council to consolidate his power and unify the Roman Empire. The following historical facts demonstrate why this belief is incorrect.

First, in 303 AD, Diocletian, the Emperor of Rome, initiated the largest and most severe persecution of Christians throughout the empire. How could Christianity unify an empire that was opposed by its inhabitants and outlawed by the government? Second, in 305 AD, Diocletian abdicated and turned the empire over to Constantius and Galerius. Constantius was Constantine's father. When his father died in 306 AD, Constantine had a legitimate claim to power, which he asserted that same year.

Third, by 312 AD, Constantine had already consolidated his power by defeating his chief rival, Maxentius. In 313 AD, he passed the Edict of Milan, granting religious tolerance to all beliefs, including Christianity. This further emphasizes the need for the protection of Christians. Thus, the Council of Nicaea was not an attempt by Constantine to consolidate his power.

So, why did Emperor Constantine convene this council? Historical records indicate that his motivation was to address a division within the church, not within the Roman Empire.

The early church was facing its first significant challenge regarding its beliefs about Jesus Christ. For the previous 250 years, Christianity had maintained that Jesus Christ was the only begotten Son of God, deity in human form. In Alexandria (near modern-day Cairo, Egypt), a man named Arius began to teach that Jesus could not be both human and divine simultaneously.

He proposed that Jesus had to be either a lesser form of deity or not truly human. This teaching became known as the Arian Heresy. The primary aim of the conference was to address this controversial teaching. Approximately 320 pastors (bishops and priests) from various regions of the Roman Empire gathered to discuss the issue. After hearing arguments from both sides, all but two affirmed that the Apostles clearly taught that Jesus was both deity (God) and human, concluding that Arius was misinterpreting the scriptures.

What scriptures were cited, you might ask?

At the conference, both sides referenced the Apostles' teachings to support their cases. How did they know what the Apostles taught? They had access to copies of books that had circulated throughout all the churches for 250 years. Both sides agreed to utilize the books that documented the Apostles' teachings and had been accepted by all Christian churches. There were 27 books, which are precisely the same ones we recognize today as the New Testament. These books became the standard, or canon, hence they are referred to as the canon today.

Once Arius was unable to convince anyone that his position was supported by the scriptures, the conference drafted a document affirming what the majority believed the New Testament scriptures taught. This document became known as "The Nicene Creed."

What transpired at this council is comparable to the contemporary scientific process employed in universities when arriving at scientific conclusions. Let's illustrate how the modern scientific system operates and draw parallels.

When a scientific researcher in a university makes a discovery, they must find a separate entity to publish their results. The university encourages this practice and actually requires professors to have multiple publications before receiving tenure. Furthermore, peers from other universities and the broader scientific community review the research by evaluating the methods used for the discovery: double-checking the math and "recreating" the experiment. If the discovery passes peer review, it is then presented at a conference where researchers from various universities gather to discuss new findings. These conferences are crucial for developing consensus within the expanding body of scientific knowledge.

Similarly, the Council of Nicaea was not a conference to create or vote on what the church believed. It was convened explicitly to address a deviation from what all of Christianity had accepted for 250 years. A new concept was being proposed, which needed to be evaluated against the backdrop of what the early church understood from the Apostles' teachings. Ultimately, this new idea was completely rejected.

A few years ago, a press conference was held in Las Vegas where a scientist claimed to have created cold fusion – a potential solution to the world's energy shortages. This announcement was quite exciting until it was revealed to be a fraud.

It may sound exciting to say that Constantine created the Bible to unify his empire, until you realize it is simply a fraud.

What Did Jesus Actually Say?

The second most popular myth today is that Jesus didn't actually say everything attributed to him in the New Testament. More specifically, this myth suggests that while Jesus taught about God, he never claimed to be God or the Son of God. It tries to convince people that the followers of Jesus created the idea of him being the Son of God centuries later. However, this notion is completely absurd.

All early manuscripts contain statements from Jesus, including his claims to be God. Additionally, other first-century authors, as early as 100 AD, wrote about Jesus and their belief that he was the Son of God. This evidence supports the idea that even his earliest followers believed he claimed to be God and accepted that claim.

Once again, the Council of Nicaea is brought up to support this myth, with claims that the debate was over whether or not Jesus was divine. This is entirely false. Both sides of the debate acknowledged that Jesus was God. The disagreement was about whether God could be human while still being God. The Arian heresy argued that all flesh and material things are evil; therefore, God couldn't inhabit human flesh without being tainted by evil. Consequently, they believed that Jesus, who was divine, could not actually be a physical being and was instead a spiritual entity, or what we might liken to a hologram. This is historically documented, as we possess manuscripts detailing the debate.

The historical evidence overwhelmingly supports the claim that Jesus asserted his divinity. While people today may not believe he was indeed God, he still made that claim.

Some may think he was delusional for claiming to be God, while others might believe he did so to deceive people. Regardless, he still proclaimed himself as God. It is dishonest to deny that Jesus claimed to be God, especially in light of the historical facts.

Suppose someone asserts that Jesus did not claim to be God, given this evidence. In that case, they are not only denying Jesus but also challenging the very process we use to authenticate ancient documents. If this process cannot convince skeptics, they will struggle to accept the authenticity of any ancient text. In simple terms: if you cannot trust the process that confirms the authenticity of the Bible, then you cannot trust the authenticity of anything.

Why Are There So Many Different Translations or Versions?

This is a genuine question. A common belief that leads to skepticism about the Bible is the existence of various translations and versions. Some people argue that these differences suggest there is no original text or that we lack knowledge of what the original said. They might also think that since the Bible was written so long ago, its content must have changed dramatically over the centuries.

Here are two important facts: There is only one original text, similar to how there is only one original Constitution of the United States, which was written just over 200 years ago. While there are many translations, they all stem from this original document.

All of the translations we have today are based on the original manuscripts; they are not translations of translations. In other words, they are all single-generation translations. When scholars create an authentic translation, they refer to the original Greek manuscripts that are accepted as the first-century writings of the New Testament. From these "original" texts, scholars produce modern-day versions.

So, why do so many different translations exist? The primary reason is the multitude of languages in the world. According to the UN, there are approximately 450 languages. If the original text is translated into each of these languages, it would result in 450 different translations. Using these numerous translations as evidence that accuracy has been lost due to multiple copies is simply unfounded. Each modern translation is made from the original manuscripts, meaning they are not copies of copies. To draw an analogy, just as the text of the United States Constitution has been translated into hundreds of different languages without anyone claiming that these translations alter the meaning of the original, the same applies to the Bible.

Additionally, English itself has many dialects and idioms, making it a complex language to learn. People in Los Angeles speak English differently than those in Boston, and the language has evolved over the centuries. For example, reading Shakespeare may leave you recognizing the words but puzzled by their meaning. This demonstrates that when the Bible is translated into modern English or any other language, it does not imply that the content is lost or altered; it simply means the new translation is based on the original, like the earlier translations.

The important fact is that we know, beyond a shadow of a doubt, what was written 2,000 years ago in the original documents. When I traveled to Washington, D.C., with my family, I visited the National Archives to see the Declaration of Independence and the original Constitution. It was a spectacular experience, albeit a bit sad, as the ink on those documents has nearly faded away. In time, one might not be able to see anything at all. However, will we doubt or question the content of these originals once the ink fades? Of course not, because the content is well documented.

Similarly, the content of the New Testament is also well documented. Intellectual honesty requires that we not doubt the authentic content of the New Testament.

Finally, even though we know what the Constitution says beyond dispute, people still argue about its meaning. These debates over interpretation do not diminish the purity and authenticity of what was written in the Constitution just over 200 years ago. Likewise, arguing about the meaning of the content in the New Testament does not undermine its purity and authenticity.

Conclusion
Let's recap the facts: scholars have developed a highly accurate process for determining the authenticity of ancient document. What is important to note is that the Bible passes all of these tests in the process far beyond any other religious text. It even passes far beyond most non-religious ancient texts like Homer's Iliad, Plato's Republic, and the plays of Shakespeare. People may choose to not believe, which is their right, but to do so on the grounds that the Bible is somehow a compromised document is simply intellectual dishonesty.

Chapter Four: Archeological Support.

Archaeology has evolved into a significant science over the last century, unveiling detailed insights into ancient cultures, peoples, and societies. Much of what we know today about ancient history stems from archaeological discoveries. The impact of this science in verifying the authenticity of ancient documents cannot be overstated.

Archaeology has a unique relationship with ancient documents. On one hand, ancient literature serves as a foundation for discovery; these documents mention cities, towns, landmarks, and monuments, guiding the search for places, identifying cultures, and locating ancient population centers. On the other hand, archaeology validates and authenticates these documents. When an ancient text refers to a city in a particular region, and archaeologists later find and excavate that city, the credibility of the document is reinforced.

The primary source for locating ancient cities, towns, landmarks, and population centers in the Middle East is the Old Testament from the Bible. In contrast, Plato's "Dialogues," one of the most renowned and complete ancient texts, describes a place called Atlantis in detail. However, Atlantis has yet to be discovered. (We still hope to find it because that would be exciting!)

The Old Testament frequently references other tribes and distant locations that have been validated through archaeological findings. For instance, it documents the histories of the ancient Egyptians, Assyrians, Babylonians, and Ethiopians, among others. It records the names of rulers, such as Ramses and Xerxes, and archaeology has uncovered their names inscribed on pyramids and stone monuments. The amount of evidence supporting these connections is substantial.

What is more interesting is the recent discoveries in support of the New Testament. Here is a list of the top 30 according to the region in which they were discovered.

Israel

Herod's temple	Jerusalem	Lk 1:9
Herod's winter palace	Jericho	Mt 2:4
The Herodium (possible site of Herod's tomb)	Near Bethlehem	Mt 2:19
Masada	Southwest of Dead Sea	cf. Lk 21:20
Early synagogue	Capernaum	Mk 1:21
Pool of Siloam	Jerusalem	Jn 9:7
Pool of Bethesda	Jerusalem	Jn 5:2

Pilate inscription	Caesarea	Lk 3:1
Inscription: Gentile entrance of temple sanctuary	Jerusalem	Ac 21:27-29
Skeletal remains of crucified man	Jerusalem	Lk 23:33
Peter's house	Capernaum	Mt 8:14
Jacob's well	Nablus	Jn 4:5-6

Asia Minor

Derbe inscription	Kerti Huyuk	Ac 14:20
Sergius Paulus inscription	Antioch in Pisidia	Ac 13:6-7
Zeus altar (Satan's throne?)	Pergamum	Rev 2:13

Fourth century BC walls	Assos	Ac 20:13-14
Artemis temple and altar	Ephesus	Ac 19:27-28
Ephesian theatre	Ephesus	Ac 19:29
Silversmith shops	Ephesus	Ac 19:24
Artemis statues	Ephesus	Ac 19:35

Greece

Erastus inscription	Corinth	Ro 16:23
Synagogue inscription	Corinth	Ac 18:4
Meat market inscription	Corinth	1 Co 10:25
Cult dining rooms (in Asklepius and Demeter temples)	Corinth	1 Co 8:10
Court (*bema*)	Corinth	Ac 18:12
Marketplace (*bema*)	Philippi	Ac 16:19
Starting gate for races	Isthmia	1 Co 9:24, 26
Gallio inscription	Delphi	Ac 18:12
Egnatian Way	Kavalla (Neapolis), Philippi, Apollonia, Thessalonica	Cf Ac 16:11-12, 17:1
Politarch inscription	Thessalonica	Ac 17:6

Italy

Tomb of Augustus	Rome	Lk 2:1
Mamertime Prison	Rome	2 Ti 1:16-17, 2:9, 4:6-8
Appian Way	Puteoli to Rome	Ac 28:13-16
Golden House of Nero	Rome	Cf Ac 25:10; 1 Pe 2:13
Arch of Titus	Rome	Cf Lk 19:43-44, 21:6, 20

This list is taken from the NIV study Bible

These archeological finds are only a small portion of what has been discovered. They are worth noting because of their direct validation of the authenticity of the Bible.

Archaeological evidence does not confirm the conclusions of statements made in ancient texts, but it can determine whether those statements are based on verifiable, factual events and places. When the data underpinning these conclusions is shown to be truthful, the statements gain authenticity.

Archaeology and Internal Consistency

There is a point at which archaeology intersects with manuscript criticism to illuminate the "believability" of an ancient document. This concept is known as internal consistency. Internal consistency focuses on the content of an ancient document and evaluates the following:

1. Chronology of Events: The goal is to assess whether the events align with the known historical record. Are the events sequential? Do they follow a logical progression? Do they tell a cohesive story? This is why Homer's *Iliad* is one of the most studied ancient documents in university courses. It has a clear line of thought, tells a story, records events that can be verified by historians, and mentions places that archaeologists can investigate. If the chronology of an ancient document does not align with the accepted historical timeline, it is considered fraudulent. While it may be interesting to study, it cannot be regarded as credible in its claims.

2. Theme: Does the document truly reflect its stated purpose, and are its claims consistent with that purpose? For example, in Shakespeare's play *Romeo and Juliet*, it is acknowledged as a work written by Shakespeare. As you read it, you can determine whether it reads like a play, if the characters are coherent, and whether there is a discernible plot, conflict, and resolution. When archaeologists discover documents claiming to be authored by Shakespeare, they look for internal consistency to verify their authenticity.

In contrast, consider the recent discovery of Gnostic texts found in Nag Hammadi, Egypt. These documents, dating to the third century, claim to be gospels—a record of a person's life. However, upon reading them, one might find that they bear little resemblance to gospels and often lack coherent content. While archaeologists regard these texts as significant finds and interesting artifacts, they do not consider them to be on the same level of authenticity as the New Testament gospels. They doubt the claims of authorship, feel that the texts do not accurately reflect historical events, and believe that the content does not represent authentic beliefs from that period.

Applying Internal Consistency to Sacred Texts

Applying internal consistency to a sacred text can either support or undermine its believability. If a sacred text does not withstand scrutiny at this level, it must be considered less reliable.

The Qur'an exhibits a high degree of internal consistency regarding its themes. It is presented as a recitation of Muhammad's visions and remains faithful to this claim. However, the Qur'an is not arranged in chronological order; the only significant divisions are commonly recognized as pre-Meccan and post-Meccan writings, which are based on where Muhammad was living when he received these visions.

Initially, in Mecca, he was peaceful, but upon moving to Medina, he adopted a more warlike stance. Without a chronological organization of the material, it is difficult for individuals to ascertain the timing of specific statements. This task is left to scholars known as Mullahs, who issue fatwas; those who issue fatwas are referred to as Muftis. This situation allows for considerable flexibility in the interpretation of statements in the Qur'an, complicating reasonable critiques regarding internal consistency.

The Vedas are particularly challenging to evaluate for internal consistency. Firstly, they lack an established chronology, being organized instead into various categories that represent different ages. Additionally, the Vedas do not maintain a common thematic focus. As shown in the chart on page 13, there is also a significant time gap between when they are claimed to have been written and the actual manuscripts available for study. This wide variability among existing manuscripts further complicates the reliability of the Vedas for scholars.

The Tripitakas have an even larger gap between their claimed dates of writing and the existing manuscripts. They do not adhere to a chronological order and fail to document events that can be historically verified. As a result, the Tripitakas can only be accepted at face value.

The Book of Mormon does follow a chronological structure; however, the claims made about North American events have never been externally verified and have generally been discredited.

In contrast, the Bible features a highly developed chronological framework that traces historical events. The New Testament is straightforward and clear, while the Old Testament is also clear but can be more challenging to understand due to its prophetic and poetic books, which were written during various kings' reigns recorded in historical accounts. Without consulting the history books first, it is easy to misplace the prophetic texts. Most importantly, the chronology in the Bible has been externally verified, with up to 90% accuracy.

One longstanding criticism has focused on the evidence for King David. If King David was indeed the most popular king in Israel, why has there been little archaeological evidence of his existence? In the early 1990s, archaeologists discovered evidence at Tel Dan supporting his existence (a good source for this information, including images of the artifacts, can be found at http://www.graal.co.uk/ houseofdavid.html).

Thanks to its rich chronology and order, the Bible is regarded as the most historically verifiable book ever written. All events recorded in the Old Testament, including ancient cities, cultures, wars, landmarks, and events such as capture and enslavement, have been corroborated.

The chronological accounts in both the Old and New Testaments cannot be disputed by any rational person. The historical and archaeological evidence not only confirms the chronological accuracy of the Biblical record but also verifies the existence of the individuals mentioned.

A prevalent misconception regarding the Old Testament is the assertion that it could not have been written during the claimed time frames because the Hebrew language supposedly did not exist before the 6th century BC. Critics argue: "There is no logical reason to believe that the Hebrew language existed prior to the 6th century BC. Consequently, the Bible cannot have been written by those who claim to be its authors."

This argument is particularly interesting; it simultaneously accepts the authenticity of the proposed authors and their time frames—which is necessary given that the early history of figures like Abraham, Isaac, and Moses can easily be determined—while attempting to discredit these authors by asserting that Hebrew did not exist at that time. This reflects circular reasoning at its worst.

Fortunately, archaeology has effectively addressed this criticism. One of the most recent discoveries comes from a site west of Jerusalem on the coastal plain overlooking the Elah Valley. Khirbet Qeiyafa existed between 1050 BC and 970 BC, during the period when Kings David and Solomon were alive. It is also believed to be the location where David fought Goliath. An archaeology professor at the University of Haifa, who is studying this site, discovered pottery from this era, further reinforcing the reliability of Biblical accounts.

Chapter Five: Truth Claims

All ancient documents discuss places, events, and people. When writing about these subjects, each document makes certain statements that can be verified as either true or false. For example, Plato writes about the lost city of Atlantis, Homer describes the Trojan War and the city of Troy, the Qur'an speaks of Mecca and Muhammad, and the Bible mentions Abraham coming from the city of Ur. The Tripitaka discusses Siddhartha Gautama (The Buddha). These statements about people, places, and events are known as truth claims, meaning they can be confirmed or disproven.

One fascinating area of study concerning ancient documents is when the claims made in these texts intersect with data from history, archaeology, and science. This point of intersection is where debates arise regarding the "believability" of a text. In other words, what occurs when an ancient document makes a specific truth claim, and that claim turns out to be accurate or inaccurate? The answer to that question is significant.

In debates, it's crucial to be well-versed in the rules of logic, as logic is a primary tool for determining the validity of a claim. Ancient scholars and scientists—such as Socrates, Plato, Aristotle, Copernicus, Galileo, and Newton—were deeply concerned with logic. In many respects, logic is the foundation of scientific discovery.

Why is this important? Many individuals who argue against the Bible employ a tactic known as the "straw man" argument. In logic, this is considered a fallacy, or a flawed argument. The straw man approach misrepresents a position by claiming that it asserts something it does not—usually something absurd—and then attacks that absurdity. For instance, some argue against the Bible by stating, "The Bible teaches that the earth is only 10,000 years old. Science has proven that the world is older than that, so the Bible must be false." However, it is essential to note that the Bible never claims how old the earth is, nor does it suggest a specific age. It merely states that God created the earth.

Intellectual honesty requires acknowledging that many well-meaning Christians use the Bible to support their beliefs. For example, James Ussher, the Archbishop of Armagh (1581-1656), postulated that the Earth was created in 4004 BC, and this theory held sway for centuries. However, other strong believers, such as Lord Kelvin—who discovered absolute zero and laid the foundation for much of modern physics—challenged this view. This highlights the importance of continually studying the Bible. As our knowledge in other areas expands, we can compare it with what the Bible teaches, allowing our understanding to grow deeper and clearer.

When evaluating the truth claims in ancient documents, we should focus on the following question: How does a specific truth claim in an ancient document align with modern knowledge?

The truth claims of ancient documents can be categorized into three groups. The first category includes specific truth claims that have been discredited. For instance, the Book of Mormon states that the North American Indian tribes are descendants of the lost tribe of Israel. This claim appears in the preface and has been modified in the 1982 and 1996 versions. It assertively claims that the lost tribe of Israel traveled to North America by boat.

Today, DNA mapping of North American Indian tribes has conclusively proven that there is no genetic correlation between the Israelites and North American Indians. (For a complete debate, see: http://en.wikipedia.org/ wiki/GeneticsandtheBookofMormon.)

This is a specific claim that has been shown to be false. To determine if a truth claim falls into this category, consider the following steps:
1. How specific is the initial statement in the ancient document?
2. How specific is the archaeological or scientific evidence regarding the claim?
3. What is the nature of the contradiction between the truth claim and the archaeological/scientific conclusions?

As you can see, logic is vital in this process. It brings intellectual honesty, and if used genuinely, conclusions can be drawn. These conclusions help decide whether truth claims fit into this category. Consequently, when an ancient document accumulates numerous contradictions, its credibility diminishes significantly.

The second category focuses on verifiable claims. When a document contains claims that can be specifically validated through archaeology or science, its authenticity increases dramatically. For instance, Homer's Iliad describes the city of Troy and its impressive walls. For an extended period, scholars believed the city was a myth, which led them to doubt the authenticity of the places mentioned in the Iliad. In 1865, English archaeologist Frank Calvert began excavating sites in western Turkey and ultimately discovered the ancient city of Troy along with the noted walls mentioned in the Iliad. These sites can be visited today. This discovery spurred new scholarship in ancient history, prompting investigations of other locations referenced in Homer's work.

On the other hand, the specific cities mentioned in the Book of Mormon that are said to be located on the North American continent have not been found by any archaeological efforts. Since none of these cities have ever been uncovered or excavated, the claims regarding their existence fall into the first category, not the second.

Another comparison involves the Hindu Vedas and the Bible. The Hindu Vedas propose that time is cyclical with no beginning or end, while the Bible describes time as linear, originating from a specific starting point and moving toward a conclusion. In 1927, George Lemaitre put forth the theory of a hot, sudden beginning of time and matter, which was later expanded upon by Hubble and validated by Wilson and Penzias in 1964. This scientific advancement caught up with the claims made in both the Vedas and the Bible, indicating that one of these perspectives must be true.

Let's follow the process with the Hindu Vedas:

Claims in the Vedas:

How specific are the claims made in the Vedas? The Vedas assert that both time and space are infinite. This notion is foundational to their understanding of God, which is viewed as the totality of all matter. Therefore, for God to be infinite, matter must also be infinite.

How specific and verifiable is the archaeological and scientific claim? The scientific conclusion that time and matter have a beginning and an eventual end was established in 1964.

What is the nature of the contradiction? The contradiction is significant. The Vedas make very specific claims about the creation of the universe, asserting that both Earth and time are infinite. This directly contradicts the scientific discovery that time has a beginning (the first cause) and will eventually come to an end.

Claims in the Bible:

How specific are the claims in the Bible? The Bible makes very specific claims that matter (the Earth) and time have a defined beginning (the first cause) and that ultimately, time will come to an end.

How specific and verifiable is the archaeological and scientific claim? These claims are highly specific and align with scientific evidence indicating that both matter and time have a beginning and an eventual end.

What is the nature of the contradiction? In contrast to many other belief systems, the claims made in the Bible are consistent with scientific discoveries regarding the nature of the universe.

The "We Just Don't Know" Category:
This category includes claims made in ancient documents that remain unverified or discredited.

The historical development of thought illustrates how this process works. As mentioned earlier, the Bible claims that the Earth and the universe have a specific beginning. During the Enlightenment (1700s - 1800s), this stance faced significant criticism from naturalists and rationalists, particularly those influenced by Darwin's *Origin of the Species*. Darwin, Huxley, and Lyell all supported the idea of an infinite Earth to justify their theories of evolution. Huxley delivered a lecture asserting that the Earth was infinite, while Lord Kelvin, known for the Kelvin scale and the discovery of absolute zero, challenged this view during a lecture at the Geological Society of London in 1869. Ultimately, Lord Kelvin was vindicated when the Big Bang theory was confirmed in 1964. This demonstrates that science had not yet advanced sufficiently to verify the truth of claims made by the Bible, the Hindu Vedas, or Huxley's geological conclusions. As more data became available, it became possible to thoroughly evaluate these truth claims.

However, there are still assertions in ancient documents that have not been verified or disproven, indicating that this evaluative process is not yet complete.

Addressing Logical Fallacies: The "Straw Hat" Argument

The "straw hat" fallacy undermines an argument using illogical reasoning. This approach involves constructing a false conclusion about a position and then attacking that false conclusion instead of the actual argument, thus making the real argument appear flawed.

For instance, the Bible not only specifically claims that God created the universe but also describes the process of creation. A common "straw hat" argument against the Biblical account is: "The Bible says the Earth is only 10,000 years old, and we know this is false, so the Bible's account is incorrect." However, as previously stated, the Bible does not actually specify the age of the Earth; it only claims that God created it.

Another "straw hat" argument focuses on the timing in the creation account rather than the process itself. The Bible states that God created the heavens and the Earth in six days. The argument mistakenly emphasizes the six-day timeframe instead of the process of creation. However, as scientific understanding of the universe's formation and the concept of time evolves, the creation process described in Genesis 1 becomes increasingly coherent. This is noteworthy because, in most other belief systems, as scientific knowledge grows, their creation narratives often become less plausible. In contrast, for the Bible, the creation event continues to gain clarity.

The final conclusion concerning Truth Claims in ancient documents is to remember they fall into different categories. Understanding the different categories allows a person to "wade through" all the different debates floating around out there. When you understand the different categories you can discern which arguments are legitimate and which arguments are not. Ultimately, you will discover that many of the arguments against the Bible fall in the third category. In other words, people attempt to take the Bible and insist it specifically makes a statement that can be scientifically proven as false.

Often, this is a straw hat argument because the Bible does not make the specific claim skeptics say it does. On the other hand, the more knowledge we gain, the more the claims of the Bible stand far and above the claims made in all other ancient documents.

Chapter Six: Historical Impact.

One way to evaluate an ancient document is by examining its Historical Significance. The goal of assessing the Historical Significance of an ancient document is to determine its "Truth Quotient," which contributes to its credibility. As mentioned in the previous chapter, all ancient documents assert truth claims that can be verified or discredited. The "Truth Quotient" evaluates the impact these truth claims had on societies and cultures. In other words, what occurred when a group of people (a society) followed the truth claims made in an ancient document? What were the core values of their society (culture), and how did they practice those values?

In 1848, Karl Marx, a German philosopher and political economist, published The Communist Manifesto. In this work, he outlined the principles of communism as a system of governance. Following revolution, some societies adopted his theory and implemented it. Consequently, what type of society did it produce? Were Marx's ideas and concepts valid, or were they invalid? By evaluating the historical impact on Russian culture, we can determine whether the truth claims in The Communist Manifesto achieved their stated goals. History has shown that the truth claims in The Communist Manifesto were inconsistent, failing to achieve the lofty objectives they proposed.

The key point is this: you can assess the legitimacy of an ancient document by examining how much it influenced a society's structure and the development of its culture. When a culture is influenced by an ancient document, the effects of the truth claims within that document reveal its true nature.

Moreover, it is revealing to consider what happens within a culture when it adheres closely to these truth claims or deviates from them. For instance, when evaluating the Vedas and the belief system they promote, what were the results for Indian culture? When examining the Qur'an, what influence did it have on societal development? Similarly, when looking at the Iliad, the Odyssey, and Plato's Republic, what kind of impact did they have on their respective cultures and societies? When analyzing the Bible, what influence did it have on various societies and their cultural development?

It is essential to note that no culture is perfect, and there is no such thing as a utopia. Therefore, promoting one culture as superior to all others lacks intellectual honesty. Conversely, in multicultural thought, no culture is deemed "better" than another, regardless of its foundational principles. This perspective insists that comparisons should not be made without being "judgmental," and conclusions cannot be drawn. If a person adopts the multicultural mindset that all cultures are equally valid, they may overlook how foundational values entered into each culture and the impact of those values. It is crucial to evaluate values as good or bad, recognizing that not all values within a culture are inherently good or bad. Thus, examining how values emerged within a culture and their effects is important.

Cultural Aberrations and Their Influence

In every culture, there are subgroups that serve as aberrations, meaning they intentionally reject the core values of that culture.

Therefore, one cannot use these cultural phenomena to assert that they are a natural implication of a text's influence on a culture. These subcultures often represent a rebellion against the prevailing cultural norms. It is not intellectually honest to use an aberration within a culture to prove a sacred text's direct influence.

India

India is one of the oldest cultures in the world, with the Indus Valley Civilization (also known as the Harappan Civilization) dating back to 2600 BC. This civilization has endured and evolved into what we now know as modern India. Historians widely agree that the primary influence on the development of Indian culture has been the religion of Hinduism. The Vedas are the sacred texts of Hinduism, and their impact on Indian culture can be clearly observed throughout the centuries.

One of the key core values in the Vedas is the belief in the infinite cycle of life and death, known as reincarnation. How one lives their current life determines their circumstances in future reincarnations. This belief has profoundly influenced Indian society, particularly through the caste system, which classifies individuals based on their birth. In this system, individuals cannot move into a higher caste within their lifetime; they must be "born" into it. Consequently, those in higher castes typically hold positions of power, wealth, and education, while the lower castes do not. It's important to note that the term "caste" in the ancient language translates to "color," implying that people with darker skin are often placed in lower castes, while those with lighter skin are in higher ones. This system of discrimination is a direct result of the core values espoused by the Vedas.

Buddhism, a sect of Hinduism, is experiencing rapid growth in Western civilization. One of the virtues that attract the Western mindset to Buddhism is its emphasis on tolerance and acceptance. Proponents of Buddhist teachings often become more tolerant and equitable in their treatment of others. However, the primary culture from which Buddhism originated is largely contrary to these values. This raises questions: Do the principles of Buddhism truly foster a more tolerant and equal society, or are they inconsistent with the daily lives of individuals within its own cultural context?

Islam

As of 2010, there are 47 nations where the majority of the population identifies as Muslim, with 23 of these countries being Islamic states. The Qur'an, along with Sharia law, serves as the sacred text and foundational legal document in these Islamic nations. Over the past 1,500 years, what kind of culture has the Qur'an fostered? What direction are these Islamic states heading in, and what values do they promote?

When evaluating these cultures, it is crucial to recognize that the Qur'an articulates a specific philosophy regarding religious faith, societal order, and political governance, as codified in Sharia law. Thus, it is reasonable to ask what a culture looks like when Sharia law is adopted and consistently applied. How are children treated in these countries? How are men and women regarded? What is the perceived value of life? What concepts of justice exist, and how are they applied?

The purpose of these inquiries is to assess the cultural impact of an ancient document. When a sacred text significantly influences a culture, one can evaluate that document based on its effects. Although the history of a culture cannot provide absolute certainty about an ancient document's authenticity, it should be a consideration when determining if the text is what it claims to be.

Western Culture

When evaluating the impact of the Bible on Western civilization, we must acknowledge two key facts. First, the Bible does not endorse the establishment of a theocracy by followers of Jesus. Throughout the last 2,000 years, authentic followers of Jesus Christ have never sought to create theocratic nations. This is true even during the time of the Crusades in the 13th century, which aimed to liberate Jerusalem. Once this goal was achieved, the crusaders departed, leaving the political class—not the Catholic Church—to establish the Latin Kingdom. The implications of attempting to create a "Latin European Kingdom" have been widely discussed, but it was never a goal of Christianity to establish an earthly kingdom.

When read in its entirety, the Bible does not advocate for a theocratic government. The primary focus of the New Testament is the establishment of a spiritual Kingdom led by the resurrected Jesus. The Old Testament, which contains the Old Covenant, is included to illustrate the inadequacy of the Jewish theocracy. Unlike Islam, this distinction is crucial when assessing the truth claims of the Bible.

Secondly, Christianity has transcended various political systems over the past 2,000 years. Therefore, it is essential to consider the broader context when evaluating the historical impact of the Bible. What are the major values of Western civilization, and how has Christianity influenced these values? Western civilization is recognized for core values that have persisted across different political systems throughout history. The strength of these core values can be seen to correlate with the influence of the Bible. Although Christianity has never tried to establish a theocracy or caliphate, its impact on societies is undeniable.

A prime example of this influence is seen in the Roman Empire. As it began to decline, the Empire split into East and West. The Eastern Empire, known as Byzantium, thrived for another 500 years, while the Western Empire continued its decline. What accounts for this difference? The answer lies in the embrace of biblical principles. While Western Rome sought to diminish Christianity's influence, the Byzantine Empire continued to uphold it, supporting and encouraging biblical principles in the daily lives of its citizens without attempting to create a theocracy.

The next important question to consider is: which cultures specifically attempted to eliminate the influence of the Bible, and what types of societies did they become? History allows us to examine how certain cultures fared once they intentionally removed all Biblical influence.

The Marxist Revolution in Russia serves as a perfect example. What kind of culture did communist Russia evolve into? Did it value its people and advance their welfare, or did it become oppressive, dehumanizing, and economically unsuccessful? The latter is true.

The primary goal of communist Russia was to eradicate any and all traces of Biblical principles to achieve its objectives. This effectively marginalized Biblical values, resulting in a dehumanizing and oppressive regime that collapsed within a generation.

Now, what type of culture is America becoming as it becomes more secular? Secularism is increasingly attempting to be the dominant influence in America today, arguing that Biblical concepts hinder the establishment of a true egalitarian society where human rights are respected and justice is blind.

One common argument is: "You can use the Bible to argue anything. There are so many interpretations that it means something different to everyone who reads it." This is simply not true. While some may misuse the Bible to support misguided arguments, these claims can be swiftly disproven. For instance, prior to the Civil War, some argued that slavery was acceptable in God's eyes, attempting to use the Bible to justify their position. This argument was quickly refuted by those committed to the integrity of the Scriptures. A notable figure, Alexander Campbell, played a significant role in dispelling this notion through his debates. He was a Virginia legislator, a tobacco farmer, and a preacher who traveled throughout the South, preaching in churches and debating anyone who claimed the Bible supported slavery. His debates focused on Biblical integrity, emphasizing the importance of adhering to the original intent of the authors. By doing so, he won every debate.

If secularism is permitted to eradicate all traces of Biblical principles from American culture, what will the culture resemble? It doesn't require a cultural anthropologist to discern the answer. Consider these questions: As secularism grows in America, is it a more just society? Is it more unified or more divided? Does it offer more opportunities for all or fewer? History tends to elucidate these issues, and it is difficult to argue that secularism has improved American culture.

Finally, consider this point regarding the rising secularism in American society. Dr. Peter Kreeft, a philosophy professor at Boston University, notes that there has never been a successful society built on or adopting moral relativism, which is one of the main tenets of secularism.

The conclusion is clear: Biblical principles make a significant difference in a culture. This impact serves as further proof that the Bible is what it claims to be—the word of God.

Chapter Seven - How to Read and Understand the Bible

Once you have developed an appreciation for the Bible and its importance, the next step is to start reading it. This can be more challenging than you might expect. You may find yourself asking questions like: Where do I start? What's the main point? What should I do if I don't understand something? These are all great questions, and with a little guidance, you will be able to read and comprehend the Bible.

The first step in reading and understanding the Bible is to put yourself in the right frame of mind. There are four principles to keep in mind to better understand what the Bible teaches.

Principle #1: Understand Your Perspective
You are reading about God's plan of love and redemption for humankind. This plan is revealed through human events that unfold over 1,500 years. Although the Bible begins with God creating the heavens and the earth, the narrative of God's plan becomes more personal starting in Genesis chapter 11 with the story of Abraham, which dates back to approximately 1900 B.C. This plan continues to develop over the centuries, culminating in the birth of Jesus Christ around 3 B.C. (It's worth noting that the monk who calculated this dating made some errors.) The section of the Bible leading up to Jesus's birth is known as the Old Testament, while the section beginning with Jesus's birth and extending beyond His death is called the New Testament. The New Testament concludes around 90 A.D. when the Apostle John recorded his vision known as The Apocalypse, commonly referred to as The Book of Revelation.

When reading about events in the Old Testament, which date back over 3,000 years, it's easy to misunderstand why God directed certain actions. For example, why would God instruct the Israelites to go to war with another tribe and eliminate them? At first glance, this may not seem to align with the overall teachings of God's character in the Bible. When encountering questions like this, remember to consider your perspective. Keep in mind that you are viewing these events from a distant vantage point and a vastly different cultural context. For instance, slavery in America was practiced until the Civil War, which was only 150 years ago. What were people thinking at that time when they believed slavery was acceptable? Some even attempted to use the Bible to justify slavery. Yet, when we read the Bible today, we often think, "How did people interpret the Bible in a way that supported slavery? I see it mentioned, but I certainly don't see it teaching that it is the right thing to do!"

Therefore, when you read the Bible and come across events or instructions that seem puzzling, remember that you are engaging with texts from a long time ago and from a culture that is often vastly different from your own. There are answers, but it requires deeper investigation to truly understand why God instructed them as He did.

Principle #2: Give it the Proper Respect

Thomas Jefferson once remarked, "Not only is yesterday's news fit only for the bottom of a birdcage, but today's as well." He didn't hold the newspaper medium in high regard. However, the Bible describes itself as the very words of God. Therefore, it is essential to approach it with a respectful attitude.

Without this respect, understanding the Bible can become a challenging task. As Paul notes, "The man without the Spirit does not accept the things that come from the Spirit of God, for they are foolishness to him, and he cannot understand them because they are spiritually discerned."

When a person reads the Bible with respect, they strive to see it through spiritual eyes. They invite the Holy Spirit to use the words of Scripture to communicate with them. Conversely, when someone who does not believe the Bible is the word of God reads it solely to critique, it may seem like foolishness. Similarly, if a person reads the Bible to promote an agenda that contradicts God's will, it may appear harsh and rigid.

It's vital for readers to approach the Scriptures with the right mindset, asking the Holy Spirit to grant them understanding and wisdom as they engage with the words of God.

Principle #3: The Events Are in Context

When reading passages from the Old Testament, you are encountering events that illustrate humanity's need for a Savior. The New Testament, on the other hand, reveals how God provided that Savior and the impact of that event on the world.

Understanding this distinction is crucial for interpretation. The Old Testament does not serve as a guide for how things should be; rather, it records why humanity needed a Savior.

Additionally, the Old Testament is written in various styles. Some books function like history, narrating events in chronological order, showcasing both the good and the bad actions of people. Other books, such as Psalms, are poetic and express the feelings of the people towards God in ancient times. In the New Testament, the four Gospels provide biographies of the life, death, and resurrection of Jesus. The book of Acts details the history of the church, chronicling its beginnings and activities in the 30 years following Jesus' resurrection.

Principle #4: The Bible is about God, not you.

The Bible is about His plan, His thoughts, His ideas and why He ultimately is doing what He is doing. John Piper once preached a message where he stated that preaching scripture is tough because ultimately it is difficult to really comprehend the mind of God. It requires concentration, effort, focus and plain old mental energy. Consequently, when I read the Bible I have to expect that I will not immediately "get it". Sometimes I need to think, reflect, and mature before I truly understand what God is saying. The Bible is a revelation of what God is doing and why. On a personal note, try as I might, I won't always understand what He was doing and why He said what He said. At times it can be perplexing, but I read and seek to understand. When I don't "get it" I pray God gives me wisdom to understand. Most importantly I pray for willingness, willingness to bend myself to what God is teaching me through the scriptures.

Often, the issue is not that I cannot understand what God has included in the Bible; it is that I don't want to believe it. In these instances, it is not wisdom I need but willingness. I need to make the commitment not to doubt the scriptures, rebel against them or reject them. I pray that understanding will come to me as I bend myself to what he has written.

Chapter Eight: Time to start reading:

To begin your journey, start with the New Testament. Although the Old Testament scriptures are included in the Bible because the Apostles used them to argue that Jesus was the Messiah, the New Testament is the more appropriate starting point. One reason for this is that beginning with the Old Testament can lead to confusion by blending Christianity and Judaism into one belief system. Therefore, as a Christian, it is best to start with the New Testament to develop a solid understanding of Jesus Christ. Afterward, you can study the Old Testament to see how it points to the Messiah—Jesus Christ.

The New Testament consists of 27 books. They are organized into basic categories:
- Biographies on the life of Jesus called Gospels.
    - Matthew, Mark, Luke, and John.
- A book of History.
    - Acts of the Apostles.
- Letters written to churches planted by the Apostles called Epistles.
    - Romans, 1&2 Corinthians, Galatians, Ephesians, Philippians, Colossians, 1&2 Thessalonians, 1&2 Timothy, Titus, Philemon, Hebrews, James, 1&2 Peter, 1&2&3 John, Jude.
    - The names of these Epistles come from the towns the letters were addressed or their authors.
- Book of Prophecy.
    - Revelation

Step One: Begin by reading the Gospel of Luke and then The Acts of the Apostles. These two books are written by the same author (Dr. Luke). Dr. Luke was a physician and a historian. Therefore, his gospel and the book of Acts are written in chronological order. These two books will give you an accounting of the life of Jesus, and then what happened immediately after His death and resurrection. This is the main focus of the entire library of books called the Bible. They are a perfect place to start and will give you the framework for understanding everything else written in the Bible.

It takes 2.5 hours for the average person to read the Book of Luke. It takes about 2.25 hours to read the Book of Acts.
If you read for 20 minutes a day. You can read through both of these books in 2 weeks.

Once you have completed these two books, read the other three biographies on Jesus (gospels): Mark, Matthew, and John.

Please note that Matthew, Mark and John are not attempting to be a chronological account of his ministry. This is left to Luke. Also, remember the target audience of each gospel. Matthew was writing to convince Jews that Jesus was the Messiah. Therefore, he quotes from the Old Testament to show that Jesus was fulfilling the prophecies made about Him in the Old Testament. Mark was trying to give a quick account on the life of Jesus and so it is very short. John was asserting that Jesus was God's only Son.

Step Two: Read the Book of Acts a second time. This is where you will learn about the origins of the church and its development in the first 30 years following the resurrection of Jesus Christ.

In the first half of the book, Peter seems to be the main character. In the second half of the book, Paul becomes the main character. Reading Acts will show you why all the rest of the letters, or epistles, were written. Acts will show you that Peter and Paul (along with others) began planting churches in various towns. The letters, or epistles, which make up the rest of the New Testament, are written to these churches.

Step Three: Read 1 & 2 Timothy, Titus. These three letters are called the pastoral letters. They were written by Paul to two of his close disciples toward the end of his ministry. Reading them gives you the idea of what is important to Jesus concerning His church. You also see how it is important to continue to grow in your faith and gain maturity.

Step Four: Read 1 & 2 Corinthians, Galatians, Ephesians, Philippians, Colossians and Philemon. These are letters written to churches by Paul. They are great to read because they show you all the issues the early church dealt with and how they overcame problems. They are also good because there is a lot of instruction on how to live your life as a follower of Jesus Christ.

Step Five: Read James. The book of James was not written by the Apostle, but by the brother of Jesus. James, the brother of Jesus, was the chief elder (sometimes called bishop) of the church in Jerusalem. He writes an excellent book for Christian living. After you have read all the previous letters by Paul, it helps to read James to round out your understanding of what it means to follow after Jesus Christ.

Step Six: Read 1 & 2 Peter, 1,2,3 John, Jude and 1 & 2 Thessalonians. These are a great grouping of books because they are not necessarily long and they show the different aspects of growing deeper in the faith. John is exceptionally good at teaching about the love God has for us and how we are called to love as His followers.

Step Seven: Read Romans, Hebrews and Revelation. These are deep books. Romans is a book of deep teaching. Paul wrote it to lay out specific arguments about how faith in God is based upon the redemptive act of Jesus Christ on the cross. Here you will discover how important faith in Jesus Christ is to God.

Hebrews was written to Jews who had become Christians but were thinking of returning to Judaism and rejecting the idea that Jesus was the Messiah. The book is an excellent in depth study of the importance of Jesus and His work on the cross. Most specifically, how God intended everything to rest on His sacrifice.

Finally, the most difficult book to understand is Revelation. Don't be surprised if much of what you read does not make sense. The reason for this is found in the very first chapter. John tells us that this book is a record of a vision or dream he had while exiled on the island of Patmos. Visions and dreams are often difficult to describe, let alone completely understand. Look for themes and general ideas as you read. Try not to get locked down in all of the imagery and detail.

Where to start reading the Old Testament

In order to understand the Old Testament, there are two concepts to keep in mind. First, it covers a huge time span- from the creation of the world to 400 BC. Second, it is a story about how God attempted to relate to a group of people. It reveals that human beings really struggle with keeping a covenant with God. As you read the Old Testament, you see people go back and forth. It is a very honest accounting of how people act and behave, and it doesn't sugarcoat anything.

In order to give you a basic understanding of the Old Testament, here is a basic timeline:

Genesis 1 records the creation of the Heavens and Earth by God.

Genesis 11 records the line of Abraham- he is called in Genesis 12 to go to the promised land. He moves from Ur (Around modern day Kuwait) to the promised land (modern day Israel). Abraham's son is named Isaac. His name is changed to Israel and his sons go to Egypt to flee a famine. They became slaves in Egypt for 400 years. Moses leads them out of slavery back to the promised land (Exodus). They lived as tribes for 400 years (Joshua, Judges, Ruth). They desire a king and the first king is a failure, so David is anointed (I and II Samuel, I Kings, 1 Chronicles). His reign starts around 1050 BC.

The books of poetry (Psalms, Proverbs, Ecclesiastes, Song of Songs) are written during this time by David and his son Solomon.

The kingdom divides in two in 930 BC. The North is conquered in 730 BC, the South conquered in 600 BC. (2 Kings, 2 Chronicles).

All of the other books in the Old Testament are written during this period of turmoil until the last book- Malachi- was written in 400 BC.

Step One: Read Genesis and Exodus. There are many good books to read in the Old Testament that will teach you about the character of God and His desire to come and save His people. The best place to start is to read the Book of Genesis and the Book of Exodus. These two books show you the earliest plan of God and His heart to connect with His creation.

When you read Genesis take note of the covenant God makes with Abraham in chapter 12:1-3. This is a significant anchor for the rest of the book. As you continue to read, look for these covenants. They are the stepping stones of understanding the plan of God. Once you have read these two books, then you will understand the Books of Deuteronomy, Leviticus and Numbers. These books have to do with the formation of the Israelites into a nation. They include the laws of how they are live and function.

Step Two: Read Joshua and Judges. These two books tell about the early history of the nation of Israel after they were set free from their Egyptian slavery and crossed the desert.. It begins with the story of Joshua, who was the general under Moses. When the Israelites entered into the Promised Land after 40 years in the wilderness, Moses did not enter with them. Joshua became the leader of the Israelites when they crossed over. It begins with the story of The Battle of Jericho.

After Joshua passed away, there was a period of 300-400 years where there was no appointed leader, or King, in Israel. The nation was sectioned off into the 12 tribes based on the land they had been given when the secured the land under Joshua. This was the time of the Judges. People appointed by God to speak for Him to the people of Israel. Here you will find the story of Gideon, Jephthah, Samson, and many more.

Step Three: Read 1 & 2 Samuel.
The reading of these two books of history will show you how King David came on the scene and what happened in his life.
It was a tremendous time of change for the nation of Israel. You begin to see how it evolves from a small, loose affiliation of twelves tribes into a unified nation of power and influence. They are excellent books when it comes to understanding the importance of King David.

Step Four: Read PsalmsOnce you understand where King David came from, then it is easy to understand the Psalms. David wrote many of the psalms as worship songs to God. The point of reading the Psalms is to feel the emotions written into the language. They are meant to move you so try and feel what the author is feeling as you read. What you will learn is that everything you feel or think is recorded in the Psalms.The Psalms are a part of the Old Testament called wisdom literature. It is a form of poetry. Other books that fit this category are Proverbs, Ecclesiastes, and Song of Solomon.

Step Five: Read Isaiah. Isaiah was the most prolific book of prophecy concerning Jesus. It is an excellent book to read to see how God planned from the beginning of the creation of the world to send His son. The primary theme of Isaiah is the holiness of God and the importance of pursuing Him in holiness. The People of Israel had rejected their sense of living in righteousness and Isaiah was called to call them back to God.

Step Six: Read the major and minor prophets. There are numerous books written by major and minor prophets in the Old Testament. Jeremiah, Ezekiel, Daniel, Hosea, Joel, Amos, Obadiah, Jonah, Micah, Nahum, Habakkuk, Zephaniah, Haggai, Zecheriah, Malachi.

The key to understanding these books is to take note of when they were written. They were written during various reigns of the kings listed in the books 1 and 2 Chronicles. One historical fact to remember is the kingdom of Israel split into two kingdoms. The North and the South kingdoms had different kings. The prophets wrote during the reign of the different kings as well as the different kingdoms.

There are other books in the Old Testament to read. Once you have read a majority of the Old Testament, and feel you have a solid understanding of the Bible, look for materials (commentaries, devotional guides, or historical studies) that will help you understand the other books of the Bible in the Old Testament. The most important fact to remember when reading the Old Testament is that it is the Old Covenant. It is a part of our Bible because it points to Jesus. Jesus is the New Covenant.

Conclusion

As you have discovered in reading this book, reading the Bible requires you to approach it through the proper frame of reference. It's all about understanding. It's an ancient document, with ancient truths. However, these truths and the principles they hold are life-changing. Therefore, you need to approach it with the proper frame of reference in order to understand the depth and breadth of its significance.

Reading the Bible has become a source of great encouragement and instruction for millions of people for centuries throughout the world. Let God speak to you through His glorious word!I hope you enjoyed learning from this book about the Greatest Book of all, The Bible. It truly is a book on which you can build your life.

About the Author
Douglas Peake. BA, MA, DMin

Douglas Peake is a retired pastor with 39 years of full-time ministry experience. He has been married to Kim since 1988.

www.ingramcontent.com/pod-product-compliance
Lightning Source LLC
Chambersburg PA
CBHW072015060426
42446CB00043B/2560